WILDFLOWERS
OF THE ROCKIES

C. Dana Bush

THE COMPACT GUIDE TO

WILDFLOWERS

OF THE ROCKIES

C. Dana Bush

LONE
PINE

The Publisher:

Lone Pine Publishing

10145 – 81 Avenue	1808 B Street NW, Suite 140
Edmonton, Alberta	Auburn, WA
Canada T6E 1W9	USA 98001

Website: www.lonepinepublishing.com

Canadian Cataloguing in Publication Data

Bush, C. Dana.
   The compact guide to wildflowers of the Rockies
   Includes index.   ISBN 0-919433-57-X

   1.Wildflowers—Rocky Mountains, Canadian (B.C. and Alta.)—Identification. I. Title.
QK203.R6B87 1989   598.13'09711   C88-091425-4

Cover Illustration: C. Dana Bush
Editorial: Mary Walters Riskin
Design: Yuet C. Chan
Layout: Yuet C. Chan, Michael Hawkins

Publisher's Acknowledgement
The publisher gratefully acknowledges the assistance of the Federal Department of Communications, Alberta Culture, the Canada Council, and the Alberta Foundation for the Literary Arts in the production of this book.

Canadian Parks and Wilderness Society
Henderson Book Series No. 15

The Henderson Book Series honours the kind and generous support of Mrs. Arthur T. Henderson who made this series possible.

PC: P4

*This book is dedicated to the plants and animals
of the Rocky Mountains, and to
my daughter Meara. May grace, and our
growing awareness and sense of responsibility,
protect these lands, so that she and
all other children can know them
as we have.*

Acknowledgements

This is my opportunity to thank the people who helped me complete this book. My thanks go to:

Eric Bailey, who originally conceived this book and who convinced me that I could do it;

E.A. (Ed) Johnson, who taught me so much about ecology and how to think, but who cannot be held responsible for any errors I may have made;

The friends and colleagues who graciously reviewed the manuscript and whose comments were so useful: Maureen Bush, Elisabeth Beaubien, Derek Johnson, Jim Posey, E.A. Johnson, G.I. Fryer, Bonnie Smith and Mrs. Beryl Hallworth;

Yvonne Arkley, whose many hours of babysitting provided the quiet time I needed to work;

My husband Dan Bilozir. Without his unassuming support and his unwavering confidence, this book would not be here in your hands.

Contents

Preface

My interest with botany and ecology began in the usual way. I wanted to know the names of the plants I saw while hiking, and I scoured books, memorizing the photographs. When I came upon a new plant, I would mutter, "I know I've seen a picture of that somewhere . . . . Now, where was it?" Only partially satisfied with this method, I studied botany in university, learning how to use a microscope and a key. Once I had learned the names of the common plants and could guess at the rest, it was a natural progression to start asking questions. Why is the paintbrush parasitic? Why does fireweed grow in such magnificent patches? Why do butterworts eat insects? Where can I find butterworts, or orchids, or lilies?

This book has had a similar evolution. It began as a simple identification guide for beginners. It was to include a hundred of the most common and showy species and would assume that most people identify flowers from pictures, not from keys. It grew to be that, and more. Rather than describing each flower with both paint and words, I have eliminated verbal descriptions. Instead I discuss the ecology of the plant. How does it relate to the world around it? Why do some plants produce poisons? How, and by what, are they pollinated? Are they pollinated at all? In this way I hope to draw you into the fascinating world of science and natural history.

This is a very small book. With such limited space, I could not include all the information about every plant. I have chosen certain plants to illustrate certain ecological principles, and although another plant may also be buzzed by bees, or parasitize its neighbours, it is not necessarily mentioned. Likewise, because of the small size of the book, it was not feasible to include a detailed bibliography. My thanks and apologies to the many authors and researchers whose work I read, and who taught me so much about ecology.

An enormous amount of knowledge of natural history comes from patient amateur observers. I have made generalizations and asked many questions in this book in the hope that some of you will be inspired to carefully observe, and to write down what you have seen. Dandelion seed heads close in the rain. Do fleabanes'? Do hummingbirds visit willow herb? If you notice anything strange or curious, let your local natural history club know about it, or drop a line to me.

Use this book as a simple guide. Look at the pictures, and if you're still interested, read the text. Then look at the flower again. And again. And again.

Enjoy.

Introduction

Our world can be seen as a web of interlocking components: the animals, plants, insects and the physical environment are bound together by an intricate lacework of relationships. Like a finely-wrought cloth of Victorian bobbin lace, each separate strand is interwoven and essential to the next. As you explore the mountains, I hope that you will become intensely aware of these relationships. My goal in writing this book, above and beyond identifying wildflowers, is to illustrate the inter-relationships among all living creatures by examining the ecology of some common, beautiful flowers, and to convey some of my sense of awe, wonder and joy in what I have found.

This exploration will start from the east. As you enter the mountains along the Bow River valley or the Athabasca River valley, the land is low and dry, with expanses of grasslands, sand dunes, lodgepole pine or Douglas fir forests. This is what ecologists call the montane ecological region: a low altitude region with extreme temperatures, low rainfall, and in this area, strong winter and summer winds. The grassland areas frequently have many prairie flowers, dusty old man's whiskers and sunny gaillardia, as well as some flowers found only in the foothills. The forests and grasslands are adapted to dry conditions and frequent fires. The first section of the book will deal with the lowland grassland species.

As you move further into the mountains, past or above the town sites, you will reach the subalpine zone. The heavily forested valleys and slopes here are colder and wetter, with deep snow in the winters. Frequently canopies of the spruce and fir forests are so dense that very little vegetation will grow under them. The plants in these subalpine forests, as well as in the montane forests, must grow with little sunlight or rain, as the thick tree branches prevent light and precipitation from reaching the ground. Look for tiny twinflowers, bronze bells, and wintergreens. At the transition between the dense conifers and the aspen grassland are open woods. There may be aspen and balsam poplar trees, roses and Solomon's-seal. Fruiting plants are common, attracting birds, mammals and insects.

Interspersed with the forests are wetlands. The shadowy brooks, tangled beaver ponds, or peaty fens are places of mystery, excitement, mosquitoes and wet feet. Here you can search for carnivorous butterworts, fragrant white bog orchids, or tiny pink elephant heads.

Climbing through the forest, the trees begin to thin and subalpine meadows appear. The meadows gradually expand, and the trees grow smaller and more scarce as you reach the tree-line or krummholz region. This zone, characterized by short twisted trees, often of extreme age, blends slowly into the true alpine. Here you will find a variety of habitats. In places sheltered from the everpresent wind, deep snowbeds form in the winter. During the spring, as they melt, they reveal glacier lilies, spring beauties, and globe flowers which bloom in the short snow-free summer. On wind-scoured slopes, exposed to the cold, wind and sun, grow the tenacious rock plants with names like rock cress and stonecrop.

In all these regions, the plants are affected by the sun, wind, snow and altitude, and interact with the animals,

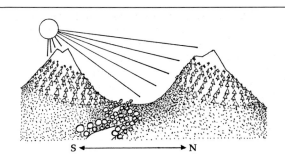

The south side of the mountains receive more sun than the north, especially during the winter. The grass generally grows higher on the south side because it is warmer.

birds and insects. Seeds are dispersed by wind, water, birds or ants. Wind, bees, flies and birds all pollinate flowers. Some plants, like pink pussy-toes, produce only female flowers which can't interbreed at all.

Knowing that certain plants are adapted to certain growing conditions means that you can predict, to an extent, where they might grow and which ones may be found together. In this book, the flowers most likely found together are grouped together in broad habitat sections. Even this arrangement is artificial, however, for a written description can never reflect the complexity and variability of a continually changing environment. Nor should we expect it to. A stream bank that seems perfect for butterworts and round-leaved orchids may not contain them for reasons unclear to us.

Sweet vetch, Indian paintbrush and strawberry are amazingly adaptable and can be found almost everywhere, but can you find them when you want to?

This is the difference between the wild and the tame: unpredictability. Therefore, if you find yourself surrounded by flowers that are not described in the appropriate section in the book, check the other sections as well.

How to use the key

Compare the wildflower you wish to identify with the key on the following pages. The page colour corresponds to the colour of the flower. The left column identifies the flower, and the top row identifies the leaves of the plant. Find one or two plants which are similar to the one you wish to identify. These may then be located by using the Index at the back of the book.

Terms used in the key

irregular	4 parts	5 parts	6 parts	7 or more	indistinguish-able
basal	alternate	opposite	whorled	fruit (berry or seed)	
entire	toothed	divided	umbel	spike	pea

A note to the reader

The number beside the colour illustration of each wildflower in this book indicates the relative size of the illustration to an average-sized plant of that species.

RED, PINK & RED-PURPLE	BASAL	ALTERNATE		OPPOSITE OR WHORLED
		entire	divided or toothed	
FOUR FLOWER PARTS		fireweed willow herb bog cranberry cowberry		
FIVE FLOWER PARTS	primose shooting star lesser winter- green dewberry	kinnikinnick red heath moss campion	old man's whiskers prickly rose grouseberry	bog laurel twin flower cut- leaved anemone sticky geranium
SIX	nodding onion			cut- leaved anemone

RED, PINK & RED-PURPLE	BASAL	ALTERNATE		OPPOSITE OR WHORLED
		entire	divided or toothed	
IRREGULAR FLOWER PARTS	calypso orchid	Indian paint-brush	elephant's head	
			sweet vetch	
INDISTIN-GUISHABLE		pink pussy-toes		
FRUIT	dewberry	cowberry	grouseberry	bunchberry
	wild strawberry	kinnikinnick	baneberry	
		prickly rose		
		twisted stalk		
		false Solomon's-seal		
		fairy bells		

| BLUE & BLUE-PURPLE | BASAL | ALTERNATE | | OPPOSITE OR WHORLED |
		entire	divided or toothed	
FOUR FLOWER PARTS		rock cress		purple clematis alpine speedwell four-parted gentian
FIVE FLOWER PARTS		alpine forget-me-not lungwort hare-bell wild blue flax	blue columbine scorpion weed	sticky geranium
SIX	blue-eyed grass			

BLUE & BLUE-PURPLE	BASAL	ALTERNATE		OPPOSITE OR WHORLED
		entire	divided or toothed	
SEVEN FLOWER PARTS		mountain fleabane Siberian aster		
IRREGULAR FLOWER PARTS	common butterwort bog violet		wild vetch sweet vetch alpine milk vetch low larkspur	
FRUIT		crowberry		

WHITE, PALE YELLOW, PALE GREEN	BASAL	ALTERNATE entire	divided or toothed	OPPOSITE OR WHORLED
FOUR FLOWER PARTS				northern bedstraw bunchberry white mountain heather
FIVE FLOWER PARTS	grass-of-parnassus sweet-flowered androsace prickly saxifrage Lyall's saxifrage one-sided wintergreen one-flowered wintergreen	alpine bistort Labrador tea	globe flower cow parsnip yarrow	mountain valerian cut-leaved anemone chalice flower spring beauty field chickweed

WHITE, PALE YELLOW, PALE GREEN	BASAL	ALTERNATE		OPPOSITE OR WHORLED
		entire	divided or toothed	
FIVE (cont'd)	wild strawberry			
SIX FLOWER PARTS	umbrella plant white camas	star-flowered Solomon's-seal false Solomon's-seal twisted stalk	globe flower	chalice flower cut-leaved anemone
SEVEN OR MORE		white mountain aven	globe flower	cut-leaved anemone
INDISTIN-GUISHABLE		woolly ever-lasting	hooker's thistle	chalice flower
IRREGULAR	round-leaved orchid	white rein orchid	late yellow loco-weed	
FRUITS			baneberry	

| YELLOW AND ORANGE | BASAL | ALTERNATE | | OPPOSITE OR WHORLED |
		entire	divided or toothed	
FIVE FLOWER PARTS	alpine buttercup	stonecrop	yellow columbine	
		yellow heath	alpine buttercup	
			cinquefoil	
SIX	glacier lily	western wood lily		
SEVEN OR MORE	golden fleabane		gaillardia	
	false dandelion	yellow mountain aven	Canada goldenrod	heart-leaved arnica
			ragwort	
IRREGULAR FLOWERS	yellow evergreen violet	yellow lady's slipper		
	late yellow locoweed	yellow paint-brush		

GREEN AND BROWN	BASAL	ALTERNATE		OPPOSITE OR WHORLED
		entire	divided or toothed	
FOUR FLOWER PARTS			western meadow rue	
FIVE	mitrewort		western meadow rue	
SIX	sticky alum-root			
SIX	bronze bells	false hellebore		
INDISTIN-GUISHABLE			pasture sage	
IRREGULAR			bracted lousewort	heart-leaved tway-blade
FRUIT	mountain sorrel	star-flowered Solomon's-seal	sweet cicely	

Grasslands

The montane grasslands are the warmest, driest and windiest areas of the mountain parks. Looking at a map, and picturing the prevailing winds, you can get an idea why this is so. The main river valleys, the Athabasca, the Saskatchewan and the Bow, lie roughly east to west: across the mountain ranges, but parallel to the prevailing western winds. In the winter, the eastern portions of these broad valleys are buffeted by the warm Chinook winds characteristic of the eastern Rocky Mountains. Rising over the coastal mountains, Chinook winds cool as the air pressure decreases, and then warm again at a faster rate as they drop into the broad eastern valleys and sweep across the prairies. Drastic temperature changes occur, raising the temperature from a frigid -20°C to a balmy +10°C in just a few hours. In mid-winter the snow melts, leaving the grass bare and accessible to the large herds of wintering elk. Come spring, the land is already dry and bare, so the vegetation must cope without protective snow cover in winter, and with little soil moisture in spring and summer.

Alternating with the unseasonably warm Chinook is the Arctic air mass. This deep blanket of cold air flows from the north down the eastern edge of the mountains, creeping into the valleys, gripping everything in its cold dry hand.

With summer temperatures occasionally reach a scorching +35°C, and with Arctic cold fronts dipping to -50°C, the yearly temperature range on the eastern grasslands can be as much as 85°C. The subalpine zone is on average colder, but doesn't have the extremes in wind or temperature.

Where are you likely to find grass instead of trees?
Grasslands are on the lower, south-facing slopes where
the drainage is good and the sun bakes the soil. There it
is too dry for even the Douglas firs. Grass grows along
the roadsides where the trees are cleared, or on thick
beds of glacially-deposited gravel, again where drainage
is good and trees can't get a foothold. Over the years a
layer of soil covers the gravel and now you find not
only some of the most dramatic flowers in the park, but
some of the most pungent.

The scent of the grasslands--the dusty rich smell of
grass, the hint of sage wafting up from our footprints, or
the smell of yarrow gently rolled between the fingers--
these evoke images of Indian religious ceremonies,
medicines, and aromatic meals. The sound of insects
buzzing and the sight of a herd of elk, or a sleek coyote,
epitomize the montane grasslands.

The grasslands meld into the montane forests of
poplar in the moister areas, and into large expanses of
lodgepole pine and Douglas fir elsewhere. You may find
some of these grassland flowers growing under the
open, park-like woods at the lower altitudes, and even
in the meadows at higher elevations.

x 1/3

x 1/3

Western Wood Lily *Lilium philadelphicum*

It is appropriate to begin with a particularly beautiful wildflower, one whose beauty may prove to be its ultimate destruction.

Showy flowers have evolved together with the insects, birds and animals that pollinate them. The diverse scents, colours and shapes of each flower act as banners or flags to attract the right pollinator.

These same characteristics also attract us. But for each flower picked, potential seeds are lost, and the balance between the energy stored in the leaves and roots and the energy needed to survive the next winter is disrupted. The plant weakens and dies. Fewer of the loveliest flowers survive each year, replaced by the less showy grasses, or the small flowered sages and vetches. The wood lily in particular has suffered for when the flower is picked, the leaves are taken as well, and frequently the shallow rooted bulb. At one time the brilliant orange of the western wood lily was commonly seen across central and western Canada. It is rarely seen now.

Gaillardia *Gaillardia aristata*

Prairie plants typically have to deal with frequent periods of drought. The dramatic gaillardia has a taproot that reaches down as much as 75 centimetres into the soil to draw up deep-seated moisture. It also has a network of fine roots in the top few centimetres which can pick up moisture from a rainfall too light to soak deep into the ground. This root system suggests that the plant should be able to survive the normal prairie dry seasons.

Old Man's Whiskers *Geum triflorum*

"Old man's whiskers," "grandfather's beard," "lion's beard," "prairie smoke": such descriptive names for this unique plant. All these names describe the appearance of the fruiting head after the petals have dropped off and the seeds have formed. The long feathery plumes on each seed were originally the styles — the female part of the flower which carries the pollen down to the ovule. After they serve their purpose in pollination, they elongate, and soft hairs grow along their length. By the time the seeds are mature, the plumes are ready to be carried by the wind or picked up in the coat of a passing coyote, to be brushed off later with the flick of a tail or a leisurely scratch.

Sticky Purple Geranium *Geranium viscosissimum*

The stickiness of the geranium comes from the hundreds of tiny transparent hairs lining the stems and leaves and at the base of each flower. Each hair is tipped with a purple gland or sac filled with a sticky scented liquid. As you touch it, the glands are crushed, releasing the oil.

Each flower petal is pale mauve to rich purple with darker purple lines radiating from the centre. Purple on purple is not conspicuous to us, but to nectar-hunting bees the lines form brilliant beacons. Bees are capable of seeing ultraviolet light, and a photograph of a geranium taken with ultra violet film shows a striking white flower with prominent black lines pointing to the nectary. Bees recognize nectar or pollen-bearing flowers by the nectar guides which show where the nectar is stored.

x 2/3

x 2/3

x 2/3   x 2/3

Harebell *Campanula rotundifolia*

The harebell (the bluebell of Scotland) belongs to the much larger group of flowers called dicots. Dicot leaves are generally net-veined. The long narrow leaves of the harebell at first glance look similar to the blue-eyed grass, but the veins have cross veins joining them together. The flower has five purple petals, and five tiny green sepals at the base. Other dicots may have four flower parts, or (like the asters) may have so many tiny flowers that you can't count the parts.

The harebell actually has two sets of leaves. Those most often seen are the long, thin, grass-like leaves. Early in the spring, the harebell also produces heart-shaped leaves on long stalks which usually wither before the flowers appear.

Blue-eyed Grass *Sisyrinchium montanum*

Hidden among the meadows and moist grasslands, a small blue star-shaped flower hesitantly peeps out to delight the eye. When not in bloom, the blue-eyed grass merges with the true grass and becomes indistinguishable, but if you slide your fingers along the stem, you'll notice that it is flattened with two distinct edges. True grass stems are round, and if you break off old, dead stalks you will see that they are also hollow.

Both the true grasses and the blue-eyed grass are monocots. This is a large group of plants which have certain easily identified characteristics. The leaves usually have parallel veins, as blue-eyed grass does, and the flower parts usually come in sets of threes or sixes, never fives. The blue-eyed grass has six similar flower parts, actually three petals and three petal-like sepals.

x 2/3   x 2/3

Wild Blue Flax *Linum lewisii*

The words linen, line, linseed, lint, and the Latin name Linum, are all said to have the same Celtic root: llin, meaning "thread." The threads referred to are the long, flexible and extremely fine fibres supporting the stem of the flax. The stems are pounded and washed to separate the fibres, which are then twisted into cords or woven into a fabric.

Annual blue flax is cultivated around the world for its strong fibres. This is what the Egyptians wove fabric from, fabric which is still found in the tombs 5000 years later. Linseed oil is made from the seed of another variety, one with shorter stems, more branches and more seeds.

Our perennial wild blue flax is less strong than the cultivated, annual variety. Although it was used by the Native people and early explorers to make rope and oil, today we value it as a beautiful wildflower.

Nodding Onion *Allium cernuum*

On open dry hillsides, or sunny grassy meadows, you will often find the nodding onion. The distinctive odour of onion is due to sulfenic acid. As you cut or bruise the cells, the volatile acid is released into the air, burning the eyes. Because of the nodding onion's amazing ability to clear the sinuses, the Blackfoot treated colds by fumigating the patient with a smudge of the bulb, and dried onion was inhaled like snuff to keep the sinuses clear. We know that garlic and possibly onions contain an ingredient effective in fighting infectious diseases, so there was good reason for these folk remedies.

Sweet Vetch *Hedysarum boreale*

If you examine the distinctive flowers, seed pods and multi-divided leaves, you can see that the sweet vetch is a member of the pea family. The roots of peas and beans have little knobs containing a specific strain of bacteria which takes unusable nitrogen from the air and converts it into a form that the plants can use. The sweet vetch uses the nitrogen (an essential fertilizer) to grow, and provides the bacteria with sugars. They both benefit so much that most peas will not grow in sterile, nitrogen-free soil unless the bacteria are present. When the sweet vetch dies, the nitrogen stored in the roots is released and made available to other plants.

Indian Paintbrush *Castilleja miniata*

The red paintbrush is one of the few flowers in the Rocky Mountains which is visited by hummingbirds. Researchers think that the paintbrushes evolved along with hummingbirds, for they are admirably suited to each other. Hummingbirds require large amounts of very sweet nectar, and they prefer flowers which are loosely clustered like the paintbrush, or single and hanging like some of the columbines.

Hummingbirds, which have very few taste buds and almost no sense of smell, can see a range of colours and are particularly attracted to red. The paintbrush has no scent, and although it doesn't produce as much nectar as fireweed, another hummingbird flower, it does provide enough. Its flowers are long and narrow and have strong tissues, so that the long bill of the hummingbird won't damage them.

34

x 2/3

x 2/3

Pasture Sage or Wormwood *Artemisia frigida*

The rich and pungent smell of sage blending with the scent of dry grass and yarrow conjures visions of free-ranging herds of elk, and eagles circling the updrafts far above. That distinctive scent comes from a volatile oil containing thujone. It's also present in the true sage, *Salvia*, which we use for cooking. Pasture sage is more accurately called wormwood.

It is not clear why plants produce these types of substances, for they're not essential to the biochemical process of growth, but it appears that they inhibit grazing. Overly-grazed prairie pastures appear rough and blue, with the round shrubs of sagebrush left behind after other grasses and herbs have been selectively eaten away. The soft pasture wormwood pictured here is not as noticeable as sagebrush but it too contains the strong-tasting and toxic chemical.

Yarrow or Milfoil *Achillea millefolium*

Yarrow also has a distinctive volatile oil, with a pleasant or offensive odour depending on your taste. Cows grazing on yarrow produce milk with a unique yarrow flavour. This can be a problem on overgrazed or damaged rangeland, for yarrow thrives on poor soils where more desirable plants cannot survive.

Yarrow also has both medicinal and insecticidal properties. In a recent experiment, the oil in yarrow killed 98 percent of the mosquito larvae exposed to it. European starlings, which reuse the same nests year after year, line their nests with yarrow and a selection of other pungent herbs. These discourage minute insects which would otherwise prey on the young birds.

x 2/3

x 2/3

Fireweed *Epilobium angustifolium*

We call the fireweed a pioneering species, for it is one that grows in newly-broken ground, and cannot survive in a crowd. The seedlings need lots of sun and bare mineral soil to grow in.

A fire, an avalanche, or road construction provides just those conditions. The light wind-blown seeds germinate in the warm soil, and the fireweed grows rapidly, covering a large area in a single year. The lush growth helps to stabilize the soil, and the roots absorb the nutrients released from burnt vegetation so that they aren't lost with the inevitable soil erosion. Within two or three years, other herbs, shrubs and trees will surpass it, depriving the fireweed of precious sunlight, and its healing flame will be quenched again. (See also Willow herb.)

Hooker's Thistle *Cirsium hookerianum*

Somehow it seems appropriate that Hooker's thistles should be pollinated by painted lady butterflies. Every few years, depending on the world weather patterns, we experience a migration of painted ladies from Mexico. Though uncommon here, they are one of the most widespread butterflies in the world. This may be because their caterpillars rely on nettles, burdock, sunflowers and thistles for food: plants that can be found on virtually every continent. They eat the leaves and build their cocoons at the tops of the plants. No doubt this harms the thistle, but when the caterpillar transforms to a beautiful black and orange butterfly; it, in turn, pollinates the flower while gathering its nectar.

x 1/2

x 1/2

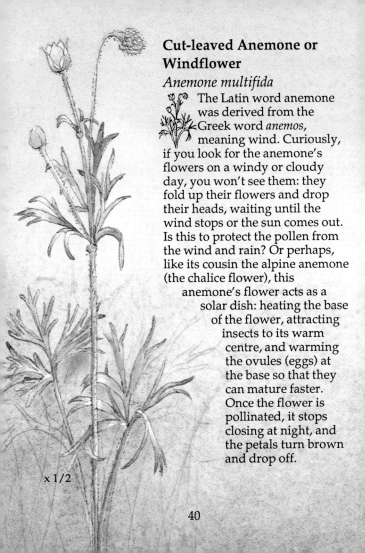

Cut-leaved Anemone or Windflower

Anemone multifida

The Latin word anemone was derived from the Greek word *anemos*, meaning wind. Curiously, if you look for the anemone's flowers on a windy or cloudy day, you won't see them: they fold up their flowers and drop their heads, waiting until the wind stops or the sun comes out. Is this to protect the pollen from the wind and rain? Or perhaps, like its cousin the alpine anemone (the chalice flower), this anemone's flower acts as a solar dish: heating the base of the flower, attracting insects to its warm centre, and warming the ovules (eggs) at the base so that they can mature faster. Once the flower is pollinated, it stops closing at night, and the petals turn brown and drop off.

x 1/2

Field Chickweed *Cerastium arvense*

 A small flower that isn't showy, but is very common and rather pretty is the field chickweed. This flower is simple — a flower with few surprises — which makes it a good plant to examine and one from which to learn.

The five white parts of the flowers are true petals and the five sepals, the smaller green leafy scales, encircle the petals. There are five styles (the female receptive stalk), with an ovary containing the ovules (eggs), and ten stamens (the male pollen-bearing parts), so each flower is both male and female. Flowers that have petals, sepals, stamens and ovaries are called complete flowers.

x 1/2

41

x 3/4

x 3/4

Pink Pussy-toes *Antennaria rosea*

The pussy-toes are great examples of incomplete flowers, as they have only female flowers. There are no male ones at all, and therefore there is no pollen. Instead, the ovules fertilize themselves and go on to produce seed — a sort of virgin birth. Sexual reproduction in most other plants involves re-combining genes from male and female flowers, and frequently different plants. Pussy-toes produce identical clones.

As you kneel on the grassy turf or gravel bed, consider that all of the pussy-toes clustered together at your knees are identical twins, or quintuplets, or more. They don't necessarily look the same, for age, wind, cold, and grazing will have their effects, but they are identical in their internal genetic make-up. The cluster three metres away, however, may be a totally different clone.

Woolly Everlasting *Antennaria lanata*

In contrast to the pussy-toes, the pearly everlasting has both male and female flowers. It is a complete flower, and produces seed in the so-called normal way.

Why the vast difference in the way plants reproduce? Clones, and flowers produced by self-pollination, do best in the short term and in the local neigbourhood. They use the "If it's good enough for me, it's good enough for you" approach. In plants that freely cross-breed the offspring will all be different, so that if the environment changes, or the seeds land far from the parents, at least some of them will survive. This is a long-term strategy.

Beneath the Trees

The flowers at the beginning of this section grow at the edges of trails, by the raw scar of an avalanche slope, or where the lower grasslands or upper meadows meet the trees. The habitats blend so that you hardly know if you're in grasslands with a scattering of trees, or in a sparse forest. Without the thick canopy of trees blocking out sunshine and rain, the undergrowth is thick and lush. Prickly rose bushes tear at your legs, and the twining vetches tug at your feet. The clear view from the air attracts small birds to the abundant fruit, with nearby trees providing shelter and safety. The dense undergrowth hides small creatures like weasels, mice and rabbits. Edges are always places of rich and abundant life. It seems that the meeting place of two different groups, whether they are cultures or ecological zones, produces a dynamic, rich joining.

Travel further, deep into the quiet still forests where the trees creak and sway in a silent wind, and patches of sunlight dart across the bare forest floor. Your footsteps are soft and muffled on the thick mulch of needles. You won't find many flowers here. The deep shade is the most obvious reason for their scarcity, but not the only one. Those tall lodgepole pines not only block out sun, but they also catch the rain before it reaches the ground. Their massive root systems soak up the soil moisture leaving little for the grasses and flowers, and then their falling needles smother tiny seedlings in their infancy.

Old needles and dropped branches litter the ground, and dead trees — fallen, or standing tall and ragged — block your path. These are home to beetles and ants, fungi and bacteria, birds and mice which work together to break down the dead material and recycle it. In this dry northern climate, however, the short summers and dry soils don't give the "decomposing crews" enough time to do it all. Litter builds up and hot dry summers set the stage for fires. Fire releases the nutrients stored in that litter on the ground, allowing them to be used by growing plants and animals.

We can't accurately predict when forest fires will occur, as there are too many environmental conditions involved. But we do know that in the past, before fire suppression was vigorously practised, these forests burned on the average of every 100 — 135 years. Although we have been taught that fires are disasters, to nature fire is neither good nor bad. Preventing all fires and causing too many fires are both disruptions of the natural order of things.

These trees and flowers have adapted to fires. Aspens produce suckers which rapidly recolonize a burn by sending up new shoots from the protected roots. Douglas fir has a thick corky bark which protects it from minor fires, allowing the surviving mature trees to rapidly re-seed a burned area. Lodgepole pine has tightly sealed (serotinous) cones from which seeds are released by the heat of a fire.

Further up the slope you will move into the cool, damp forests of the subalpine. These halfway forests are wetter than the lower montane, but the rain frequently takes the form of a light and pleasant drizzle rather than a prairie downpour, and the winter snow falls deep and undisturbed. In these damper areas, the forests change to white spruce, alpine fir and Engelmann spruce. A thick carpet of feathermosses, clubmosses and lichens cover the ground, and here you'll find the shade-loving plants like the delicate twinflower, bunchberry, bronze bells, and the tiny, almost unseen, mitrewort.

When walking up a wooded trail and emerging in an open meadow or avalanche trail, take the opportunity to look across the valley and compare the treelines. South-facing slopes receive more hours of sunlight than do those which face north, especially in winter; they have a longer, drier growing season. Western slopes are buffeted and dried by Chinook winds, while eastern slopes benefit from the early morning sun, and are sheltered from the wind. At lower altitudes, the warm dry south-facing slopes may be blanketed with Douglas fir forests for a considerable way up their sides, while the north slopes may have thick white spruce forests growing at an equally low altitude. At timberline, the trees will extend much further up a south-facing slope than up a corresponding north-facing one.

A striking example of this (and there are many) occurs on the Saddleback trail above Lake Louise. The lower portion of the trail winds through a dense, shady spruce forest, broken by progressively younger avalanche slopes. Near timberline, the spruce and fir give way to larch and then to a lush open mountain meadow. On a warm summer's day, an alpine meadow often appears idyllic, but a sudden snow storm can force the ground squirrels into shelter, and drive you down the other side of the ridge. On the warm southeast side, protected from the wind, you'll often find a thick spruce forest, and it's only then that you appreciate that the meadow exists because the climate is too harsh for trees.

The treeline is another broad edge where the plants and animals of the forests blend with those of the meadows and alpine rocks. As you climb through the spruce and fir forest, savouring the pungent scent of the alpine fir and enjoying the refreshing coolness of the forest, the trees begin to thin, the ones remaining becoming more twisted and stunted the higher that you go. These are krummholz trees, and will be discussed in the section on high meadows and rock slopes.

Northern Bedstraw *Galium boreale*

Northern bedstraw also spreads by rhizomes, so a cluster of plants is usually found together. The stem is slender and distinctly square, with leaves in whorls of four. The main use of northern bedstraw was as a source of dye. The leaves yield a yellow colour and the roots, when combined with wood ashes and a high-acid berry — perhaps cranberry or crowberry — give a beautiful scarlet hue which was used on porcupine quills.

Canada Goldenrod *Solidago canadensis*

Canada goldenrod grows in circular colonies about a metre across, though very old colonies up to 30 metres across have been found in the prairies. All goldenrods within the circle are clones of one another, and are connected to each other by underground stems called rhizomes. Many species send out these shoots (quack grass and aspen trees are two well known examples) but in most plants the rhizome connecting the two plants breaks off, leaving two individual plants. In the goldenrod, this connection is maintained, so that the whole colony acts as one individual.

If a goldenrod shoot comes up in a poor environment, the whole community will share in the misfortune, transferring toxins and nutrients back and forth through the rhizomes. The damaged plant will be fed and nurtured by the others, and though the whole community may become stunted, all members will usually survive — a sort of floral socialism.

x 2/3

x 2/3

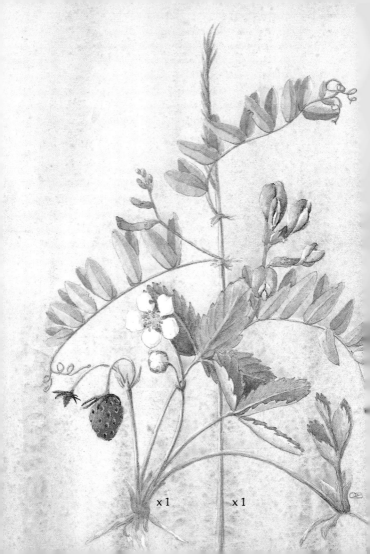

x 1   x 1

Wild Strawberry *Fragaria virginiana*

Strawberries avoid the either/or question of reproduction by taking both approaches. They flower and produce seeds in the usual fashion, but they also produce cloned plantlets on the end of long runners or stolons. Stolons are similar to rhizomes: rhizomes are underground horizontal stems, while stolons are above-ground horizontal stems. Follow a strawberry runner and you will see it go up and over rocks and gravel, reaching out to find a patch of bare earth in which to root a new plantlet.

The strawberry is difficult to place in any particular zone, for it grows nearly everywhere, from the lower montane forests to subalpine meadows. In the shade it produces masses of leaves with few fruits. At the edges of the woodland trails where the sun shines through, or in open meadows, it fruits abundantly.

Wild Vetch *Vicia americana*

Along the edges of the woods where the forest overlaps the meadow, the vegetation is thick. In spring, wild vetch transforms this mat into a tangled riot of purple blooms.

The tangling is due to the tendrils at the tip of each set of leaflets, the tendril actually replacing the top leaflet. These tendrils reach out until they contact a young aspen tree, a fence wire, or an old yarrow stalk. The sensitive tip begins to curl around the stalk or wire as the rest of the tendril corkscrews, pulling the whole plant towards the support.

Late Yellow Locoweed *Oxytropis monticola*

The yellow locoweed is an extremely dangerous plant for grazing animals. In good weather when grass is abundant, most animals avoid locoweed. If a drought sets in or if there are too many animals for the pasture, they may be forced to eat it or starve. Once they've eaten it, however, they develop a craving for it and even if they are provided with healthy food, they will gorge on locoweed until they die. Locoweed poisoning begins with general lethargy and a vacant stare progressing to muscle spasms, inability to walk or eat, and eventually death. Bees react in a similar way and beekeepers have lost whole hives when the blooming alfalfa fields were mown before safe alternative bee flowers bloomed. (See milk vetch for identification.)

Yellow Paintbrush *Castilleja occidentalis*

The paintbrush is a parasite. Under the soil, its roots spread until they make contact with another plant. Fastening onto the roots of the neighbouring plant, the paintbrush pulls water and minerals directly from it. The invaded plant grows more slowly, and may wilt from lack of water while its parasitic neighbour thrives.

Some paintbrushes can grow alone, but many of them cannot live without a host plant nearby. They will even live off one another, one plant becoming healthy and strong, the other stunted and weak.

Paintbrushes need the extra water that the host plant provides. If a paintbrush is picked, it wilts immediately: another good reason not to pick wildflowers.

x 1

x 1

x 1/5   x 3/4

Cow Parsnip *Heracleum lanatum*

Cow parsnip is a tall plant with stalks up to 2 metres high and with leaves as broad as dinner plates. The flower heads are bouquets of tiny white flowers in flat broad heads, and each flower that is pollinated turns into a flat, striped seed. The seeds are eaten by all sorts of animals and birds. An adventuresome researcher collected grizzly feces and discovered them to be full of cow parsnip seeds. When the seeds were tested for viability, it was found that they grew better after having been processed through a bear. The seeds did better yet if they were left to freeze over the winter. This kind of seed dormancy is common among northern plants. It means that they're not likely to germinate before spring, nor will they be destroyed by being eaten.

Star-flowered Solomon's-Seal *Smilacina stellata*

The star-flowered Solomon's-seal is not nearly as big as the cow parsnip. It stands about shin-high and grows in large stands of thickly clustered plants. Researchers dug up one cluster of them and discovered that all the shoots belonged to one plant — there were 26 metres of rhizomes connecting 58 different shoots! When a plant spreads this way it becomes very difficult to tell which shoot started as a seedling, and how old the plant is. The researchers estimated that this plant was 17 years old, but it could have been much older. It appears that very few star-flowered Solomon's-seal plants actually sprout from seed.

Yellow and Blue Columbine
Aquilegia flavescens and *A. brevistyla*

Columbines come in a wonderful array of shapes and colours, each of which attract different pollinators. The blue columbine has short spurs and is visited by those bees which can easily reach the nectar at the end of the short spurs. The yellow columbine is pollinated by long-tongued bees which can reach the nectar in the long curved spurs. However, short-tongued bees cheat and chew a hole in the end of the spur to steal the nectar without pollinating the plant.

Western Meadow Rue *Thalictrum occidentale*

A close look at the meadow rue may reveal both male and female plants. The male plant has tiny purplish sepals that fall off early, no petals at all, and its yellow stamens dangle down like fringes on a Victorian lamp shade. The flowers on the female plants have little purplish styles that stick out at odd angles. Eventually these flowers will develop into clusters of hard dark fruits.

The meadow rue is well adapted for wind pollination: there are no petals to get in the way and the pollen-loaded stamens hang down and swing in the breeze. But when the wind carries the pollen to the female flower, how does it manage to land on the tip (the stigma) of that very small style? The flowers are aerodynamically designed so that minute air currents swing around the flower and drop their loads near the stigma. In addition, just to make sure there is contact, the pollen is positively charged and the stigmas are negatively charged: the attraction pulls them together.

x 2/3

x 2/3

x 2/3

x 1/3

x 1/3

Purple Clematis *Clematis occidentalis*

Clematis vines curl in the same way that vetch does, except that instead of a tendril at the tip of the leaf, the whole leaf stalk curls. Young shoots twirl as if searching for something to hold onto. As soon as an object is touched, the searching movement ceases, and the vine begins to curl. Friction on one side of the sensitive new leaf stalk causes the tissue on the opposite to grow faster, forcing the stem to curl more and more. Once the stem is coiled it becomes very hard and tough.

Prickly Rose *Rosa acicularis*

The prickly red pincushions found on many rose leaves are galls. They are caused by gall-wasps which lay their eggs inside the leaf. When the egg hatches, a small white legless larva emerges and, safe in the gall, it grows and eats and grows until it pupates. Breaking out, the adult wasp flies away. The advantages to the wasp are obvious: it has free housing and food. The plant seems to be in a losing position: it's being eaten and distorted. But the gall is the plant's way of protecting itself from the larva. The larva is encased in a hard shell, where it may be safe but it can't move and it can't do much damage. Together they have evolved, each becoming more specialized until the gall-wasp can't live without the rose, and the rose puts up with only minor damage.

Calypso Orchid or Venus's Slipper
Calypso bulbosa

In early spring, just as the pale green aspen leaves unfurl, the calypso orchid emerges from the thick mat of half-rotted leaves and needles on the forest floor. At the same time, a new crop of young bumble-bees emerges, searching for nectar and pollen.

The young spring bees haven't yet learned to recognize the true nectar-bearing plants. Attracted by the scent and by the yellow hairs on the top of the slipper, they land, looking for food. Pushing their heads into the pouch, they rub their backs against a tightly-bound package of pollen on the upper inside of the flower. When they back out, they carry the pollen, but no nectar, with them to the next flower.

This strategy probably only works a few times before the bees become wary of flowers bearing false promises. However, for the pollination of the orchid, a few times is all that's necessary.

Yellow Lady's Slipper *Cypripedium calceolus*

The toe of the yellow lady's slipper is really a petal shaped into a pouch. Bees enter through the hole at the top, searching for food. They can't climb back out for the edges of the hole curl inwards, and small hairs on the sides point down. The bees bumble about inside, depositing pollen on the stigma in their search for the exit. At the rear of the pouch is a transparent window which shines light on two small exit holes. To get to the holes, the bees must squeeze past the anthers, picking up more pollen on the way out.

60

x 1   x 1

Twisted Stalk *Streptopus amplexifolius*

In the shade of thick trees, the leaves of twisted stalk and fairy bells float serenely above the forest floor, gently swaying like ripples on a pond.

Why are they spread out flat like this? The leaves on all plants are arranged so that each leaf receives the most amount of light possible. Usually leaves grow in a spiral arrangement up the stem so that one leaf never completely covers another. Deep in a forest where the light is diffuse and dim the stems stretch out flat, exposing every leaf to the patches of sunlight dancing through the trees.

x 1/2

Fairy Bells *Disporum trachycarpum*

Fairy bells have a soft velvety fruit, rather like a peach in texture. You can see the bulges of the three clusters of seeds inside.

Smaller birds eat the flesh off the fruits, leaving the seeds behind. Larger birds eat the whole berries. To survive being eaten by a bird, a seed must be tough. It must withstand being pecked, swallowed, ground in the crop, regurgitated or excreted. Most berry seeds have a tough outer coat to ensure survival.

Birds with very heavy beaks can actually crack the seeds and digest the whole thing. In this case the plant must take a chance that at least a few seeds will fall, unnoticed, on the ground.

x 1/2

Lungwort
Mertensia paniculata

The lovely drooping bells of the lungwort begin as tightly furled pink buds, turning blue as they expand. The chemical anthocyanin gives the flower its colour, and when the cell sap is acid, it stays red. As the buds open, the carbon dioxide that was trapped in the bud escapes and the cell sap becomes alkaline, turning the flowers blue.

Many insects can't see shades of red. Ignoring the closed pink buds, they pollinate the ripe blue flowers and fly on. Once the flowers are pollinated and turn pink again, the insects ignore them.

x 3/4

x 1/2

False Solomon's-Seal

Smilacina racemosa

At the ends of long graceful
stalks hang succulent red berries
dotted with purple. Fruits are the
plant's way of having its seeds
distributed, and their colours and positions
can tell us which animals are likely to eat them.

Most insects don't see red, and they concentrate
mainly on soft fruits which have fallen on the ground.
Most mammals have poor colour vision. They will eat
red berries, but won't search them out. Red berries on
flexible branch tips are almost certainly eaten by colour-
sensitive birds; the ruffed grouse is one. The patterns of
purple dots help identify these berries as false
Solomon's-seal rather than the striped star-flowered
Solomon's-seal or red baneberry.

65

x 2/3

x 2/3

Heart-leaved Arnica *Arnica cordifolia*

Arnica grows in both shady and moderately sunny spots. When it grows in the shade, it has large thin leaves, often light green in hue. Arnicas growing in the sun are noticeably different; they have small, thick leaves and appear to be a darker green. The surface of the leaf is rougher and the root system is more extensive.

If you think about the conditions, the differences are easily understood. Shade plants need to capture as much light as possible; hence the large (and thin) leaves. Sun plants have all the light they can use. Large leaves aren't necessary so they become thicker and dark green. Sun plants dry out faster though, so a larger root system to pull in moisture, and a rough leaf to limit evaporation, are in order.

Bunchberry or Canada Dogwood
Cornus canadensis

Bunchberry grows in the shady forests, where it develops slowly and rarely blooms. When campsites are built, the lower branches of the trees are often stripped so that visitors can walk beneath them. This lets in just enough extra light to give a boost to the bunchberry and it starts blooming. This is one reason why the plant is so common in forested picnic areas and campsites.

The bunchberry's endurance is also due to its rhizomes or underground stems. Each rhizome tip has a dormant bud. While the main shoot is flourishing, the bud remains dormant but if the main shoot is pruned or is burned in a forest fire, each bud starts growing again, sending up new shoots.

One-sided, and Lesser Wintergreens

Orthilia secunda and *Pyrola minor*

Have you ever hiked up a mountain trail and felt as though you were climbing backwards in time, from summer to spring and then to winter? At the bottom of a valley the wintergreens, the raspberries and the strawberries have already set seed. Climb up the trail for an hour and you can find wintergreens in full bloom, nestled in the moss and leaf litter. Hike on up the mountain and you're lucky to find the evergreen leaves poking through last winter's snow.

The same thing happens as you move north. If you have a strong urge to see a certain flower in bloom (as I sometimes have), and you find you've arrived in Banff too late, driving north along the Ice Fields Parkway towards Jasper will frequently reward you with flowers in every stage of the cycle.

This change in blooming times is known as Hopkin's Law. For every degree of latitude or, for each 122 metres change in altitude, the flowering dates of a given species of flower will change by four days. Hence the higher up or the further north you go, the later the flowers will bloom. The flowering date at the north end of Jasper should be 12 days later than in the southern parts of Banff (3° latitude x 4 days), and the flowering dates at Sunshine Village should be 26 days later than at Banff townsite (800 metres elevation gain).

Left: One-sided Wintergreen
Right: Lesser Wintergreen

68

x 1   x 1

Mitrewort or Bishop's Cap *Mitella nuda*

The miniature lacy mitrewort flowers blend in with the feather mosses like spider webs in a spruce tree, unnoticed until the light hits them the right way.

The easiest way to find them is to look for the light green, kidney-shaped leaves lying almost flat on the ground.

Once you have found one, look closely at the flowers. Each flower has 5 plain sepals, and 5 finely wrought petals resembling tiny antennae. In the centre are 10 stamens. (If you only count 5, you've found one of the other, rarer species of mitrewort.)

The name mitrewort or bishop's cap is a description of the shape of the seed capsule.

Heart-leaved Twayblade *Listera cordata*

Heart-leaved twayblade is a plant of cool acid soils, where the moss grows thick and feathery.

Centuries ago, during the last ice age, sheets of ice crept down from the north, covering the prairies, the valleys and the hills with thick layers of ice. Only the peaks of the mountains and some hills escaped their scouring, and only plants that grew further up the mountain sides, or south of the ice sheet, survived.

This little orchid, with its ability to live in cold damp soil, survived high in the Rocky Mountains. When the glaciers retreated, twayblades migrated north to Alaska, the Hudson Bay region and east to Labrador.

The flowers range from greenish yellow to dark green or purple.

x1

x1

Kinnikinnick or Bearberry
Arctostaphylos uva-ursi

Intermingled with the twinflower is bearberry, another evergreen, mat-forming plant. The Latin name *Arctos* means bear and the Greek *staphyle* means bunch of grapes. *Uva-ursi* also means bear berry. You may be happy to note that bears do indeed eat these berries, as do grouse.

This plant has also acquired a number of uniquely Canadian names. Kinnikinnick was originally an Indian name which came from Eastern Canada. It referred to a mixture of herbs used as tobacco, including native tobacco, bearberry and assorted other herbs. Fur traders brought the mixture and the name to Western Canada, but the name soon referred to just bearberry, perhaps because real tobacco was rare.

In a neat verbal turn-around, the coastal Indians named it sacacomis, after the smoking pouches habitually carried by the Hudson Bay clerks. Sac means bag, and commis means clerk, in French.

x 1

Twinflower *Linnaea borealis*

Vast carpets of twinflower, their long creeping stems a metre or more in length, cover the shady forest floor. Each stalk bears two fragrant flowers, standing small but proud.

Twinflower is a northern flower (the name *borealis* means northern). In a vast circle around the pole, in areas such as Northern Europe, Siberia, and Canada, the little flower thrives. Its first name, *Linnaea*, was taken from Karl Von Linnaeus, a Swedish botanist who probably named more plants, animals and minerals than any other person in our history. He had explorers send him specimens from Africa, India, the Orient and of course Western Canada (Prince Rupert's Land). The twinflower was one of his favorites.

x 1

Grouseberry *Vaccinium scoparium*

Grouseberry, with its jointed broom-like branches and flat bottomed berries, is common and easy to identify. The fruits are related to the blueberry but are much smaller, and tart.

Outside the parks, bird hunters search out areas with grouseberries, knowing that they will find grouse with their crops stuffed with berries. Late in the season after the berries have hung in the sun and fermented a while, the grouse show distinct signs of inebriation.

Bears also graze on grouseberries, consuming the whole plant: berries, leaves and all. If you see fresh bear scat in the autumn, make some noise, survey the scene carefully to ensure that the scat isn't really fresh, and then take a look. It's often full of partially digested berries.

x 3/4

Cowberry or Mountain Cranberry
Vaccinium vitis-idaea

Cowberry is an evergreen plant. In the early spring, just as the snow melts, the sap begins to move and the plant warms up. Within two weeks, the old leaves are working at full capacity to capture solar energy and convert it into substances the plant can use. New leaves start producing two weeks after the leaf buds begin to open, and they all continue to photosynthesize until late in fall.

Unlike the evergreen cowberry, deciduous blueberries (like grouseberry), can't start photosynthesizing at all until after the new leaves have opened up. They may lose several weeks of sunny warm weather before the soil thaws completely. They make up the time by doing more work in a shorter period; they photosynthesize at a faster rate. If you measure the amount of work done by the leaves, both the deciduous grouseberry and the evergreen cowberry come out equal by the end of the season. They just accomplish it at different rates.

x 3/4

Baneberry *Actaea rubra*

To come across a branch loaded with shiny succulent red or white baneberries is an open invitation to pick them. Don't. Although small birds and animals eat these berries, they are poisonous to us.

The baneberry is the only plant I know of that produces red or white berries, but never on the same plant. Both the red and the white form are the same species, and there isn't any discernible difference in the size or the number of fruits or seeds. We have no real idea why the different forms co-exist.

Sweet Cicely *Osmorhiza depauperata*

Sweet cicely belongs to the parsley family. It is closely related to the wild cow parsnip, the poisonous water hemlock, and common carrots. All these plants have small white flowers radiating from one central point forming a fairly flat bouquet of flowers called an umbel. These flowers attract any available insect: it's an open-house concept of pollination. Any sized fly, wasp, bee or beetle is welcome - so if you're interested in insects, start looking near the sweet cicely.

The fruits are dry and slender, appearing on the ends of long graceful stalks like the swollen feelers of a moth. The stalks radiate out from the central point just as the flowers do. They have a very distinctive licorice scent, and were used as a breath freshener. They are not very common, so refrain from picking them.

x 2/3

x 2/3

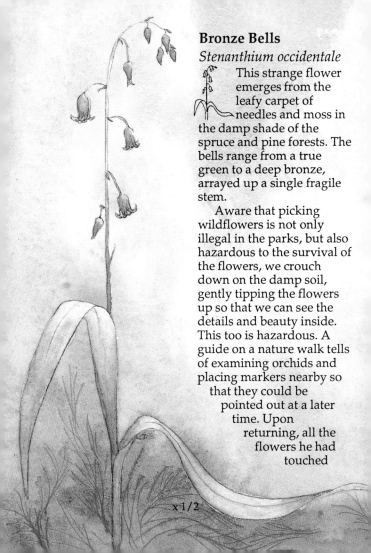

Bronze Bells

Stenanthium occidentale

This strange flower emerges from the leafy carpet of needles and moss in the damp shade of the spruce and pine forests. The bells range from a true green to a deep bronze, arrayed up a single fragile stem.

Aware that picking wildflowers is not only illegal in the parks, but also hazardous to the survival of the flowers, we crouch down on the damp soil, gently tipping the flowers up so that we can see the details and beauty inside. This too is hazardous. A guide on a nature walk tells of examining orchids and placing markers nearby so that they could be pointed out at a later time. Upon returning, all the flowers he had touched

x 1/2

had been nipped off! He guessed that the salt and oil on his fingers attracted the small animals, which ate the stems. Try using a small stick if you want to examine flowers closely.

One-flowered Wintergreen *Moneses uniflora*

The one-flowered wintergreen is one of those rare delights one sees at the side of a trail, or along a shaded brook. The flowers are always single, and the stem has a loop at the top that bows the flower, keeping its face cast towards the ground.

There is no pigment that makes flowers white. Rather, like snow, the colour is formed by the reflection of sunlight from myriads of tiny air pockets in the petal (or snow bank) scattering the light in all directions, without absorbing any one colour.

Some white flowers also reflect ultraviolet rays, making it easier for the insects to see them. However without special lenses and photographic film, we can't tell the difference.

x 1

Wetlands

Let's begin our walk at the edge of a stream, meandering through a subalpine meadow. The bank is grassy and damp where the water seeps into the field. Beside the log which bridges the stream, black mud oozes. This is a marsh: slow running water, rich in nutrients, with grass and other moisture-loving plants growing in the thick black mud. This is the place to look for clusters of richly-scented white bog orchids, deep purple bog violets or little pink elephants.

The landscape opens into a shallow bowl, allowing the water to collect in large open areas. As you walk, the ground gets spongy and you no longer feel mud beneath your feet. Sedges, rushes and occasionally cotton grass abound, their grasslike stems reaching up to your knees. You are in a fen now, with sedge peat thick beneath your feet. The plants growing here are perpetually wet, with almost no oxygen at the roots. The deep water and lack of oxygen prevent most decomposing bacteria from working, so when an old sedge dies, it slowly drifts to the bottom of the pool, building up a soft absorbent layer of sedge peat. The peat gets deeper and deeper, slowly compressing with the weight of the years. It's a slow process which may build only 200 centimetres of preserved, packed plants in 1000 years.

At the edges of the fens, where there is a little more soil available and the drainage is somewhat better, you'll often find tiny pink primroses, shooting stars, round-leaved orchids and the carnivorous butterworts.

In places where the water is still and quiet, the ground is sometimes carpeted with a soft layer of feather moss. The water here is slightly acidic. All plants produce acidic by-products as they grow. Usually in the Rocky Mountains, the acids combine with the abundant calcium in the water (these mountains are mostly limestone — a calcium-rich rock) which neutralizes the acid. The product is washed away, leaving neutral or alkaline waters in the streams, marshes and fens. But in places with very still water, the calcium gets used up, the products aren't washed away, and the acid accumulates along with the peat. This isn't really a bog, because true bogs have sphagnum moss growing in the acid cold water, and very little sphagnum moss grows here. But we do find a lot of other bog species — plants that do particularly well in slightly acid conditions. You might find the spring-loaded swamp laurel, the small but tasty bog cranberry, the crowberry, and Labrador tea.

Plants can grow under a variety of conditions, so you may find any number of these plants growing in any damp spot. You may also find plants from the woodlands or meadows such as grouseberry, kinnikinnick, or perhaps grass-of-parnassus. You will find that rubber boots and insect repellent are essential equipment for a walk in the wetland.

Elephant's Head *Pedicularis groenlandica*

In the marshes and the fens, you may stumble on one of creation's great practical jokes — tiny pink elephants growing wild in the Canadian Rockies. Are we to be reminded that mammoths and elephants once roamed here?

These plants are pollinated by bees. The stamens with their pollen-loaded anthers are tucked into the head of the elephant, while the style is in the trunk. The bee lands on the trunk, the tip of which curves up alongside the bee to touch its back. Then holding onto the ears and the forehead for stability, the bee vibrates its wings, shaking the pollen into the air and onto the chin (the lower petals) of the elephant. Collecting the released pollen from the elephant's chin, and from its own belly, the bee returns to the hive with its bounty.

White Bog or White Rein Orchid

Habenaria dilatata

The name rein orchid describes the long strap or rein-like spur: the hollow tube that projects down from the base of the flower. This is where the nectar is produced and, because of the length of the spur, can only be collected by hummingbirds or by long-tongued insects such as bees, butterflies and moths. My guess is that it is pollinated by night-flying moths, for it has all of the necessary characteristics: a bright white flower that can easily be seen at night, a strong scent to attract them, and a long narrow tube offering nectar.

Look for these wonderful orchids in the marshy areas along stream banks in subalpine areas.

x 2/3

x 2/3

Bog Violet *Viola nephrophylla*

Violets have two kinds of flowers. There are the showy ones which are pollinated by insects and produce offspring with a wide variety of characteristics. Out of sight at the base of the leaves is a second set, which look like tightly-closed green buds. These too are flowers, but they never open and are not pollinated from another plant. They pollinate themselves in secret, and produce offspring nearly identical to the mother plant.

Scientists engage in continual speculation about the sexual habits of plants. Is it better to produce a great number of very different offspring through "normal" sexual reproduction and bet that some of them will find just the right spot for their needs? Or is it better to produce duplicates by self-pollination or by cloning, and assume that what is good for the parent will still be good for the offspring? The violet does both.

Dewberry, or Arctic Raspberry *Rubus arcticus*

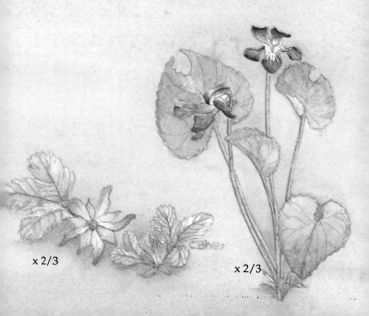

The leaves of dewberry are very similar to the wild raspberry, with their slightly rough surface and toothed edges. In fact the dewberry is a dwarf raspberry. The fruits are bright red and fragrant, but they are rarely found by us as squirrels, mice and grouse soon eat them.

Raspberries are notorious for the numerous seeds embedded in the fruit. They're the ones that get stuck in your teeth. In botanical terms, each seed with the fleshy part around it is a single fruit called a drupe. Raspberries and dewberries are clusters of fruits.

x 2/3

x 2/3

Bog or Swamp Laurel *Kalmia polifolia*

Bog laurels are flowers worthy of close inspection. Note that each flower has ten little pouches recessed into the petals. When the flower first opens, one stamen lies nestled in each little depression. When a bee, searching for nectar, lands on the laurel blossom, its heavy body triggers the spring-loaded mechanism and ten stamens snap forward, bombarding the bee with pollen.

The entire plant, including the nectar, is poisonous. Honey made from swamp laurel is also poisonous. Fortunately it is so bitter that it is seldom eaten.

x 1

x 1

Small Bog Cranberry *Oxycoccus microcarpus*

These lovely hanging pink flowers develop into tiny sour red berries — small bog cranberries. The large bog cranberries cultivated in B.C. , Nova Scotia, Quebec and Ontario are what we generally serve with our Thanksgiving and Christmas turkey. The small cranberries provide winter food for a number of animals such as muskrats, white-tailed deer and sharp-tailed grouse.

In the wild, some seeds are carried in the gut of game birds and shore birds to a suitable growing site. Others over-winter on the plants, and during spring flooding, their buoyant berries detach and float down-stream to a new site. Commercial berry growers take advantage of this natural buoyancy. On cranberry farms, the fields are flooded, then the submerged plants are raked by hand or beaten with mechanical harvesters. The berries float to the surface, and are suctioned up and processed.

Dwarf Canadian or Bird's-Eye Primrose
Primula mistassinica

The flowers drawn in the circles are cross-sections of primroses from different plants. Notice that on one flower the style (the dark part in the drawing) is very long and the stamens (orange) are clustered at the bottom of the tube. On the other plant, the stamens are attached at the top where the throat of the flower opens up, and the style, at the tube's base, is very short.

When a bee lands on the long-styled flower, he thrusts his head in to reach the nectar and receives a dusting of pollen on the front of his head. Then he buzzes over to the next plant and dives in again. This time the top of his pollen-coated head contacts a short style. The flower becomes fertilized, and this time the bee flies away with pollen on the back of his neck. This pollen will contact the tip of the next long style, fertilizing yet another flower. As flowers on the same plant will all be either long- or short-styled, never both, this system ensures cross-pollination.

Shooting Star *Dodecatheon pulchellum*

The shooting star has a curious way of spreading its pollen from flower to flower. The flower hangs with the pollen-loaded stamens dangling below. A bumble-bee grabs the tip of the cone and swings around so that it is hanging upside down underneath the flower. It then rapidly beats its wings, vibrating the pollen right off the stamens. The pollen drifts down in a yellow cloud and settles on the furry belly of the bee. You can watch a bee "buzz" a tomato flower in your garden the same way.

x 1   x 1

x1   x1

Round-leaved Orchid *Orchis rotundifolia*

Many plants (like the ubiquitous strawberry) can grow under a broad range of conditions. Others, like this orchid, need a delicate balance. A full ripe capsule may produce millions of minute seeds, but only a tiny proportion survive to produce more flowers. Successful seeds must fall on cool wet soil that has a specific soil fungus. The fungus grows with the orchid roots, helping the orchid to absorb nutrients from the acid soil. Seeds landing on soil lacking the right fungus do not survive.

Common Butterwort *Pinguicula vulgaris*

The butterwort is one of the few carnivorous plants in the Rockies. From a distance it looks like a tall violet, but the flat yellow leaves are distinctive. The edges of the leaves are curled up like flat-bottomed boats and are covered with tall stalked glands sporting tiny drops of liquid glue. Trapped in the glue may be myriads of tiny insects. Another layer of glands exude an acid liquid laced with digestive enzymes in which the hapless insects are drowned and digested.

We think this is a way of compensating for a nutrient-poor environment. Even though the running water in a fen is continually washing fresh nutrients in, the water is frequently very alkaline, with large amounts of calcium dissolved from the limestone rocks. Calcium reacts with phosphorus, an element essential to the growth of all plants, changing it into a form that the plants can't use. Butterwort consumes insects to obtain the phosphorus, nitrogen and other nutrients that it can't get from the soil or water.

x 2/3

x 2/3

Labrador Tea *Ledum groenlandicum*

Knee high and sparsely leaved, Labrador tea can be most easily identified by its distinctive leaves. Turn a leaf over and you'll see that the edges curl inward so they look somewhat like a small rowboat. The underside of the leaf is covered with a dense rust-coloured fur.

Labrador tea grows where the soil is poor, acidic and wet. Its presence indicates that special care may be needed to prevent soil compaction by heavy machinery. Bogs and fens can be seriously harmed by compaction from vehicles and even by hikers. This is one of the reasons why you'll often find parallel logs (corduroy roads) placed on a wet path or even raised walkways and bridges along some heavily-used trails in the parks.

Crowberry *Empetrum nigrum*

Crowberry is a low shrub with tiny pink flowers which in turn form small black berries. The berries are edible, and provide a valuable winter food for birds and animals.

Occasionally you'll find a boggy area of mossy hummocks surrounded by pools of still water. In the centre of each hummock grows crowberry, bog cranberry or Labrador tea. Moss has an amazing ability to hold many times its own weight in water. A hummock can grow high above the water table and still be very wet, and it's also more acidic in the centre than in the open water. Each little hummock has its own set of microclimates, from wet and weakly acidic at the edge, to damp and acid in the centre. Crowberries grow in the acid range best suited for them.

Mountain Meadows and Rock Fields

To run in a mountain meadow, to watch the squirrels harvest buttercups or an eagle soar on an updraft — this is close to heaven. But the heaven here is transitory. The growing season may be as short as two months, with a mean summer temperature of only 6 °C. Warm spells rarely last more than a week, and then the slopes are again accosted by freezing winds and snow. Plants and animals growing here must have distinct adaptation abilities for survival.

The first things I notice as I climb through the deep forest into the patchwork pattern of meadows and open woods are the trees. Known as krummholz, a German word for "twisted wood," these trees give a clear indication of the harsh wind and snow patterns. The short summers hinder the maturation of the new growth of needles, allowing the bitter winter winds to dry out any exposed shoots and to scour their branches with shards of wind-blown ice. Huddled behind a boulder or buried in snow, the surviving branches grow slowly and appear to reach away from the wind, staying low to the ground. Some of these contorted flag-trees are hundreds of years old, but scarcely a metre tall. Higher up, even these trees reach their limits of tolerance, and fail to grow.

In the deep snowbeds grow glacier lilies, chalice flowers and buttercups. Protected from the winter winds by a deep blanket of snow, they must grow quickly once the snow has melted to take full advantage of the brief season of warmth and sun. The season is so

Krummholz Trees

1. *Safe beneath the snow, a young tree grows slowly until its top bud exceeds the height of the snow pack.*
2. *The next winter, the exposed tip is killed by the cold and the wind-driven ice. The rest of the tree remains protected.*
3. *Each spring the tree sends up a new top shoot which is killed during the winter. Any exposed branches on the windy side are also pruned by the wind. Though the tree may be hundreds of years old, it will rarely exceed the winter snow level.*

short that flower buds may form two years before they bloom, and plants use the food stored in their roots to begin growing before the snow has even melted. You will find plants pushing their way through the melting snow, already in bloom. In a particularly bad year, when the snow doesn't melt at all, many of these plants live on their stored reserves, buried under the snow until the following summer's sun brings respite.

On the tundra and scree slopes the conditions are very different. The plants here have to deal with almost constant drought. Many have long tap roots reaching deep into the soil to garner as much moisture as possible. The winter winds howl across the slopes, picking up snow and dumping it on the lee side of the mountains, leaving these plants unprotected for most of the winter. Undaunted, they don their own protection. They grow low, in small rosettes, dense mats, or round cushions. They jealously guard the small bits of soil and dead leaves from the wind, keeping the precious nutrients safe under a thick layer of leaves. The leaves themselves are small and round, giving the least wind resistance possible, but with minimal overlapping so that each leaf has maximum exposure to the sun.

The leaves also have their own protection. Some, like the golden fleabane, may be hairy, protecting the leaves from moisture loss and trapping the heat in a thick fur coat. Others, like the stonecrop, have thick, waxy leaves. The low profile and protected leaves actually warm the plant on a sunny day. The centre of the plant may be as much as 5 °C warmer than the surrounding air temperature.

If you gently lift the leaves of a stonecrop, you will find a number of roots growing at each cluster of leaves. Most of the alpine plants propagate by vegetative means; sending up new shoots from underground stems (rhizomes), rooting from above ground stems, or forming bulbils, rather than relying on seeds as the plants growing at lower elevations do. With the short growing season frequently preventing seed production (it may take two years just to produce a flower) and the slim chance of survival that a new seedling encounters, other options must be used. Often a trade-off ensues. If its flower buds have been set in the previous year, the yellow avens — when faced with an extremely dry summer — may quickly bloom, set seed and go dormant without producing any new shoots or leaves that year. Moss campion may not bloom for ten years, and twenty-five years may pass before it flowers profusely. A careless step or a plucked snowfield flower may destroy many years of painstaking growth.

x 2/3

x 2/3

Glacier or Avalanche Lily
Erythronium grandiflorum

As you trudge across a soft, melting snowbank, leaving pink and blue footprints behind, you don't expect to find flowers in full bloom. So the sight of a dozen glacier lilies with their canary yellow flowers reflected in the snow can bring surprise and delight.

Glacier lilies have corms, a swollen underground stem somewhat like a bulb. These store a rich supply of carbohydrates during the summer and fall. In the early spring, before there is enough warmth or sunshine to provide food through photosynthesis, the plants draw on this stored food supply, blooming before their leaves are fully developed.

Chalice Flower *Anemone occidentalis*

Picture a radar dish sitting in the middle of a snow field, tracking a satellite, collecting, focusing and concentrating radio signals to the very centre of the dish. Now look at the broad open blossom of the chalice flower and imagine it as a sun dish, tracking the sun from horizon to horizon, focusing and collecting the heat rays in the very centre of the flower. This solar furnace can actually raise the flower's temperature anywhere from 6 to 10°C, depending on the type of flower and the amount of cloud cover. It warms the reproductive organs, giving them a little boost toward maturity. It also provides a warm sheltered spot for small insects to gather, basking in the sun and munching on the abundant pollen.

Inset: Tow-head baby seed head of the Chalice Flower

x 1/2

x 1

Mountain Valerian *Valeriana sitchensis*

Sometimes late in the summer, a walk through an alpine meadow will assault your nostrils with a pungent, almost rank, odour. It is difficult to locate, for the distinctive smell seems to permeate the entire meadow. The source is a volatile oil which comes from the roots of the valerian. The Europeans are familiar with a similar plant, the common pink-flowered valerian. Their legends claim that the odour is particularly attractive to rats, and that the Pied Piper of Hamelin used a little valerian along with his pipe to entice the rats away. Maybe he used it with the children as well, for it is well known for its effective tranquillizing and sedative effects.

Alpine Buttercup *Ranunculus eschscholtzii*

The flower of the buttercup is sometimes confused with the yellow flower of the cinquefoil. They both have open flat flowers with large amounts of pollen, but the buttercup has that wonderfully distinctive shiny surface on the petals. The yellow pigment is concentrated in a thin layer of cells on the surface of the petal. Beneath it lies a layer of cells filled with dense white starch grains. The light passes through the yellow layer and is reflected off the white starch in the same way that light passes through the transparent pigment on a water colour painting, strikes the white of the paper below and is reflected back to your eye, brightened and enriched. In contrast, the base and the back of the petals have a different structure and pigment, and so are not glossy.

Lance-leaved Spring Beauty *Claytonia lanceolata*

If you were a grizzly bear and therefore had the Park's permission to dig bulbs and corms for food, spring beauty would be the one to search for in that hungry time at the end of winter. Below ground, the stem extends downward for several centimetres and swells up into a round storage organ called a corm. It looks similar to a bulb, but it doesn't have the fleshy leaves surrounding it. All the food is stored in the stem itself. The corm supplies the plant with a sure food supply in early spring before the leaves are able to manufacture food, so the plant can flower as soon as the snow melts, earning it the name of spring beauty.

The corms are also eaten by rodents, and you'll sometimes come across elk, deer or sheep grazing on the succulent leaves and flowers.

Globe Flower *Trollius albiflorus*

The globe flower and the alpine flowers on the preceding pages all require a deep bed of winter snow for survival. Protected from the cold winds and blown ice by a thick snow quilt, they lie warm and safe until spring. In the centre of the snow bed, the snow may not melt until very late in the year.

You will sometimes see a series of concentric rings of plants with globe flowers, glacier lilies and buttercups around the edges where the snow protects them in winter but melts early enough in summer for them to flower. In the center of the snowfield, where the snow sometimes lingers year round, you'll find a soft bed of damp moss.

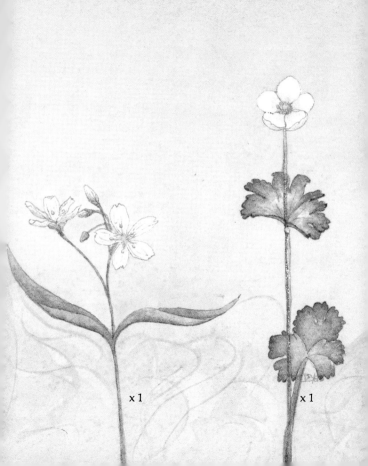

x 1   x 1

Mountain Fleabane *Erigeron peregrinus*

The elegant mountain fleabane turns to seed early in the season. The fruit is shaped somewhat like a shuttlecock or badminton birdie, with a single-seeded dry fruit at the base and a cluster of stiff hairs surrounding the dried remnants of the tiny floret. An animal scurrying past the tall stiff stalk of the fleabane may brush against it, jerking the stalk and catapulting the fruits through the air. Like a thrown dart, or a served shuttlecock, the seeds fly free before diving, right side up, to the earth. (See also Aster.)

Bracted Lousewort *Pedicularis bracteosa*

Bracted lousewort is closely related to elephant's head and to the white, contorted lousewort. You can see the similarity in the fern-like leaves and the strange flower. The boat-shaped leaf (bract) beneath each flower is the source of this one's name.

Though the three louseworts rarely grow together (elephant's head needs wetter ground and contorted lousewort needs drier ground than the bracted one), they do grow close enough that a bee may visit all three species in one forage. Since this means that each plant may come in contact with the pollen of the other species, hybrid crosses of the plants could in theory be produced. Since we don't find any hybrids, we can assume that there is some kind of chemical or physical block that prevents the pollen of one flower species from fertilizing another.

x 2/3

x 2/3

x 1   x 1

Alpine Forget-me-not *Myosotis alpestris*

Notice the bright blue of the forget-me-not with its contrasting yellow centre. Like a carefully calculated advertisement, your eye is attracted to the bright cluster of flowers, then quickly focuses on the yellow centre. The same thing happens to bees. The contrast between the blue and yellow serves as a banner telling them that this is a flower with nectar and pointing to the spot where it may be obtained. Pollen that is carried by bees has tiny teeth, or comes in sticky packages, which adhere to the bees' fur. The smallest pollen grains are usually wind blown, and the average bee pollen is slightly larger. Forget-me-nots are the exception: they have the smallest pollen grains we know of.

Lyall's Saxifrage *Saxifraga Lyallii*

Curious about the small size of alpine plants, ecologists transplanted certain alpine species to sea-level to see what would happen. Although they sometimes grew larger than they would on a mountain top, for the most part they remained smaller than their sea-level cousins. As they normally grow at lower temperatures, they flower earlier in the spring and may have difficulty dealing with hot weather. Though extremely hardy in their native environment, they are easily choked out by the vigorous growth of their lowland neighbours.

Occasionally you may find Lyall's saxifrage growing as far down as the montane forest, but it will always be in some protected moist spot, along a wet stream bank, or at the edge of a pond. These plants are susceptible to drought, and cannot grow in dry areas.

False Hellebore
Veratrum eschscholtzii
Low Larkspur
Delphinium bicolor

 How can a plant that cannot run and hide protect itself from predators? Producing poisons is one solution.

Both the ankle-height larkspur and the very tall false hellebore are poisonous plants. They each produce toxic alkaloids which can make you very ill and may be fatal.

These poisons are natural by-products of plant growth. Somewhere along the evolutionary track, a plant evolved with a slightly different chemical that herbivorous insects or animals could not tolerate. Left alone to grow in peace, the plant thrived and reproduced. Soon, most of the plants in that species produced the toxin, and the predator had to adapt or perish. Because of their short life cycles, insects can evolve rapidly, and in short order at least one

x 1/10

108

group of insects responded by metabolizing the toxin and went back to eating the plant. The plants then synthesized a new toxin, and the insects adapted to it: back and forth in an evolutionary see-saw. Sound familiar? The farmers and gardeners with their army of chemicals are playing the same game. We produce a toxic chemical and the insects adapt, so we make another. Unfortunately, we produce far more than a community of false hellebore or larkspur does, damaging other parts of the environment in the process.

The larkspur lives in moist meadows and open woods from subalpine to alpine. It is pollinated by bees. The false hellebore is found in broad flat meadows in the subalpine where the snow lies late, or where a meandering stream seeps through the soil. The stalks are covered with small green flowers and may be as much as two metres tall.

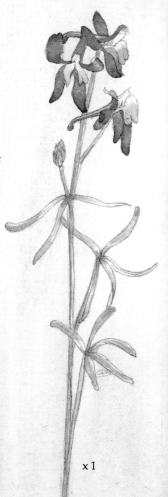

Left: False Hellebore
Right: Low Larkspur

x 1

Mountain Sorrel *Oxyria digyna*

The mountain sorrel is portrayed in this picture with its fruits — small round seeds with bright red paper-thin wings on either side. The wings of the fruits, the edges of the leaves, and the slender soft stems, glow with a rich red light. The red colour is from a chemical called anthocyanin, which occurs in all plants, but is usually hidden by the green chlorophyll. Alpine flowers and sorrel in particular have more red then other plants. Because the atmosphere is thinner on the mountain tops, ultra-violet radiation is stronger. This is what is responsible for the bad sunburns that mountain climbers get, and it also damages leaf tissue. The red colour acts as a filter or a sunscreen to protect the tissues in the plant.

Fringed Grass-of-Parnassus *Parnassia fimbriata*

Grass-of-Parnassus grows in moist crevices and stream banks where meltwater and rainwater keep the soil damp all summer long. These soft-stemmed, thin-leaved plants must have damp soil to survive. In the slightest drought, they wilt. They bloom in midsummer in the warmth of the sun, well after the spring flowers.

The five petals are fringed, giving a lacy appearance, and there are five white stamens and five sterile stamens, called staminodes. The bright yellow staminodes glisten with small amounts of nectar, attracting all sorts of small flies. Attracted by the fake stamens, they don't bother eating the pollen on the real stamens, though they probably pick some up on their body hairs inadvertently.

x 3/4

x 3/4

Alpine Milk Vetch *Astragalus alpinus*

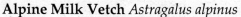

Flowers in the pea family are sometimes difficult to tell apart. The wild vetch is identified by the tendrils at the leaf tips. The easiest way to tell the other vetches apart is to wait until the seed pods form. Milk vetches and locoweeds have pods like garden peas: a simple pea pod with no constriction on it (though it may be furry or puffed up). If the pod has a waist between every seed, then it is a sweet vetch.

The next thing to look at is the keel or the lower part of the flower. It is formed by two petals meeting at the bottom, and looks like the keel of a boat. Milk vetch has a rounded end on the keel, while locoweed has a sharp pointed end.

x 2/3

x 2/3

Yellow Evergreen Violet *Viola orbiculata*

Have you ever noticed that no matter where you sit, you get ants in your lunch? They are everywhere. Violets take full advantage of this.

Mice, voles, chipmunks and other small animals will gladly eat violet seeds. If the seed capsules opened slowly and let all of the seeds drop to the ground close to the mother plant, a persistent mouse could eat every seed produced. Instead, the dry capsule snaps open into three parts, throwing seeds for three metres in every direction. Then the ants get to work. Each seed has a little parcel of fatty food on the outside of it. The ants collect the seeds, eating the fatty part and throwing the intact seed onto the refuse pile at the edge of the nest.

Consider that ant's nest. It is composed of fine soft soil with few weeds. It has deep mineral soil blended with organic top soil, with a little ant dung mixed in: wonderful potting soil. The germination rate and survival of the small seedlings is far better for those seeds collected by ants than for those seeds left to sprout alone. Who benefits, the ants or the violets? Maybe both!

(See also Bog Violet.)

White Mountain Heather, and Yellow and Red Heaths

Cassiope mertensiana,
Phyllodoce glanduliflora, P. empetriformis

These three heathers, the white mountain heather (*Cassiope*), the yellow or glandular heath (*Phyllodoce glanduliflora*), and the red heath (*Phyllodoce empetriformis*) are frequently seen growing together, intertwined and covering the ground with a coarse and prickly mat.

Occasionally a hybrid will be found. A hybrid is an offspring of two different species, in this case the red and yellow heaths. The heath hybrid looks similar to both the yellow and red heath, for it has a pale rose flower that's shaped like a narrow bell, and may or may not have glands. It's only found where both parents are present, which indicates that it can't reproduce itself. There are a number of reasons why this may happen. There may be genetic or chemical barriers to pollination. Or it may be that insects which are attracted to it do not come in contact with the pollen and the stigmas in the right manner. Still another explanation may be that the flower is so oddly shaped that insects aren't attracted to it at all.

These flowers often grow in and around the stunted trees at timberline. They need a good layer of moist acidic soil, so they must be protected from the winds in the winter. Take a walk around the meadow until you find the windward side of the mountain. This is the side that the wind hits first, and it's usually the west side in the Rockies. Here the soil is thin and rocky, which generates a different set of plants. Back where the heathers grow, the wind is less, so the soil can accumulate without being blown away and the winter snows mean moisture in the spring.

2/3

x 2/3

x 2/3

x 1

x 1

Alpine Bistort or Knotweed
Polygonum viviparum

Viviparum means 'live birth.' Though some bistort plants in Alberta have fertile flowers, others have sterile flowers clustered at the top of the stem. Below the flowers, looking very much like flower buds, are bulblets. These are baby plants, clones of the parent, which start growing while still on the stalk. When they fall off, they quickly establish themselves because of this head start.

Sweet-flowered Androsace, or Rock Jasmine
Androsace chamaejasme

When hiking in southern Alberta, I climbed over a windy ridge onto a hot rocky slope. The rocks looked barren and bleak from a distance, but up close I found a sparse but rich covering of alpine plants in full bloom, and an unmistakable scent of tropical jasmine. On my hands and knees on this precarious slope I finally identified the source: the sweet-flowered androsace.

As you kneel down to smell these plants, notice how the wind blows less strongly near the ground. We hunch down to get out of the wind, and so do alpine plants. They grow low, in mats or cushions or rosettes like these. A rosette is a cluster of leaves at the base of the stem. Each leaf is precisely positioned to shade the one below as little as possible so sun can be absorbed, and the leaves lie close to the ground to avoid the cold dry wind.

x 1

x 1

Four-parted Gentian *Gentianella propinqua*

Four-parted gentian is one of the rare annual alpine plants. To go through a whole cycle in one season, it must be able to grow rapidly. The seeds must germinate early and easily. Neither deep nor thick roots are necessary; as it doesn't have to survive the winter, more energy can be diverted to leaves and flowers. The gentians at lower altitudes, where the season is longer, have several side branches and flowers on taller stalks. To save time and energy, the alpine versions are stripped down: they have fewer branches, fewer flowers and smaller over-all size.

The flowers never quite open up. What looks like closed buds are actually open flowers with the four petals touching in the centre; hence the name four-parted gentian.

Alpine Speedwell *Veronica alpina*

Alpine speedwell is a perennial plant, as are most of the other alpine flowers. The growing season is so short that annual plants are extremely rare. There is no time to sprout, grow, flower and set seed in one season; instead, alpine plants like speedwell spend many years establishing themselves and building good strong root systems before they start to flower.

Many alpine plants begin forming their flowers one year and sometimes two years before they actually bloom. Whether a particular year is a good one for seeing alpine flowers depends on many factors, one of which is what the weather was like the summer before when the flower bud was being formed.

x 2/3

x 2/3

Ragwort or Groundsel, and Siberian Aster

Senecio streptanthifolius and *Aster sibiricus*

When you pick a daisy, you don't just pick a flower; you pick a bouquet. The garden daisy, the asters and the ragworts are composed of many small flowers clustered together in a single head. In these composite flowers, there are frequently two different types of flowers grouped together. In the ray flowers (the purple ones in this aster) all of the petals are joined together to make one long strap-like petal, often with a bend in it to make it project out like the rays of the sun. In the tube flowers (the yellow ones in the centre of a daisy-type flower head), the petals are joined together to make a slender tube.

Different species have different colours and arrangements of these flowers. As you can see, this aster has many bright purple ray flowers. The ragwort has a few yellow ray flowers. Dandelions are made of ray flowers only, and thistles have tube flowers only.

The *Erigeron* or fleabane is the one flower most likely to be confused with the asters. There are so many different shapes and colours of asters and fleabanes that only the most expert botanist can identify them all. The asters tend to have fewer ray flowers, generally five to fifty, while the fleabanes have more than fifty. Asters bloom in late summer at low elevations, while fleabanes bloom early and are usually in seed by midsummer. Of course at higher elevations they frequently bloom together.

Left: Ragwort
Right: Siberian Aster

121

×2/3

×2/3

Umbrella Plant *Eriogonum umbellatum*

The flowers of the umbrella plant are dry and paper-like, pale yellow at first, turning pink as they age. The flowers produce nectar and large amounts of pollen so they are regularly visited by bees, beetles and flies who collect the pollen and nectar.

Pollen is a rich source of protein, with some sugar and fat thrown in. All animals need a quantity of protein, and pollen is easily accessible to small creatures. Beetles climb right onto the top of the umbrella plant to eat the pollen grains, grinding them as they eat to break open the tough walls. Bees can digest them without chewing.

Sticky Alumroot *Heuchera cylindrica*

Little research has been done on alumroot. It is an American plant, growing in the temperate regions; there are no Asian or European alumroots. It was used by the Indians as an astringent and as a remedy for diarrhoea.

Any time I've seen it, there have been tiny insects crawling in and out the flowers and along the stems. The sticky glands on the stems and flowers must produce an oil or nectar that attracts the insects. Why? What kind of insects are they? Are they only there when the flower has just opened and the pollen is fresh, or do they always hang about? What do they do?

These are the kinds of questions that an observant amateur naturalist can answer. Too often we assume that science must be left to those in universities and laboratories, but there are still many things for the rest of us to discover and share.

x 1/2   x 1/2

False Dandelion *Agoseris glauca*

Agoseris is often called false dandelion. True dandelions and *Agoseris* look very similar, but the blue-green leaves of the *Agoseris*, sometimes covered with white fur, aren't toothed or divided like true dandelions. *Agoseris aurantiaca* looks similar but has orange flowers.

The most striking similarities to the true dandelion are the flowers and the milky juice in the stems. This thick white liquid, called latex, is a suspension of different chemicals: by-products of the growing plant which are too big to pass out through the cell walls. Because plants don't excrete their wastes like we do, they must store them in the leaves or roots, or in this case in latex in the stem. It was once thought that the latex was used to heal wounds, but most plants heal well enough without it. It probably protects the plant from grazing animals but, curiously, latex in plants evolved before there were animals to eat them.

White Camas *Zygadenus elegans*

In the centre of each petal on the white camas there is a green heart-shaped gland. If you find a plant which has more flowers in a compact cluster, and round glands on each petal, then you've found a death camas. Both plants are considered poisonous, though the white camas is not as potent. Most deaths have occurred because of mistaken identity. In southern Alberta the bulbs have been mistaken for blue camas, an edible bulb. They have also been confused with onions, although they don't smell or taste anything like them.

Mountain Cinquefoil *Potentilla diversifolia*

Cinquefoil means "five-leaved" in French. If you look at the leaves, you can see that each one is shaped rather like a hand, with five or sometimes seven divisions branching out from the centre. These leaves are usually covered with soft white down, giving it a silvery appearance.

It's easy to confuse cinquefoils with buttercups, for they both have five-petalled yellow flowers of about the same size. Buttercup petals are very shiny and the plant usually has smooth leaves. Cinquefoils have dull yellow flowers and though some — like this species — grow in moist meadows, most are found in drier places.

Scorpion Weed *Phacelia sericea*

When I announced my intention to include scorpion weed in this book, several naturalists advised that it was rare in Banff and Jasper. Later that summer while hiking at the top of Mount Norquay, I rounded a bend and discovered myself on a hillside surrounded by scorpion weed. There were hundreds of plants, all in full bloom. The following summer I returned and could not find so much as a leaf to show that they had ever been there.

What happened to them? Scorpion weed is a short-lived perennial with seeds that germinate easily. The plants probably grow slowly, hidden among the other herbs. In a year with just the right weather conditions they suddenly burst into vivid bloom, covering the hills with their fuzzy flowers. Setting seed, they die, and the cycle begins again.

x 3/4

x 3/4

Willow Herb or Broad-leaved Fireweed

Epilobium latifolium

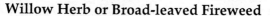

Like the closely related fireweed, the willow herb is capable of both cross-pollination (pollination from other plants) and as a last resort, self-fertilization. If you examine a stalk in full bloom, you may be able to see that the upper flowers are male and the lower ones are female. Willow herb blooms from the bottom up: each flower is first male, producing pollen, then turns female,

x 3/4

x 3/4

making ample amounts of nectar and then seeds. Honeybees, bumble-bees and butterflies visit the female flowers at the base of the inflorescence first, collecting the nectar and working their way up the stalk. As they reach the pollen-bearing male flowers the nectar runs out, and so they fly to another inflorescence carrying a load of pollen from the upper flowers to fertilize the lower female flowers on the next plant. If cross-pollination is unsuccessful, the female parts will lengthen and open, coming into contact with the remaining pollen and fertilizing themselves.

Yellow Mountain Avens *Dryas drummondii*

Driving along the Icefields Parkway, you pass the Sunwapta River meandering back and forth between thick beds of gravel. All along the edges of the river and in the gravel at the edge of the road, you can find carpets of yellow dryads.

Wind or water carries the dry fruits with their long silky tails to a fresh bed of gravel at the base of a glacier, along a river or road. There the plants develop into thick mats that can spread up to two or three metres across. The roots have nodules containing nitrogen-fixing organisms which provide the plant with its own fertilizer. What an advantage when you're trying to grow in a gravel bank! The leaves form dense mats low to the ground and though the wind may blow, or the rivers may flood, that thick mat of leaves holds tight to the little bits of dirt and humus trapped within, slowly covering the gravel with good rich soil.

Moss Campion *Silene acaulis*

Big roots, small plants. When a seedling of moss campion settles in to grow, the first few years are spent making roots. In five years the part you see may be smaller than a bottle cap, but the central taproot can reach 1.0 — 1.5 metres into the mountain. This massive root holds the plant in place while the shifting sliding scree moves around it. In a more stable area, the central root reaches down between the rocks to pull water up and the plant spreads across the rocks.

x 1

x 1

Sometimes you will find a cushion of moss campion a metre across. A plant as large as this is more than twenty-five years old. The branches underneath are tough and resilient, but they'll still break if you step on them. Unlike stone crop or saxifrage, broken shoots of moss campion will not grow new roots. They just wither and die.

These plants are designed to be tough — they can handle cold, wind and drought. They can't withstand the pressure from lug-soled hiking boots.

Lyall's Rock Cress *Arabis lyallii*

The flowers of rock cress are simple, with four petals in the shape of a cross and long narrow seed pods standing erect at the end of the stem. When the seed pods are dry, they split into two long sections leaving a thin dividing membrane behind. The seed pods and the four-part flowers are typical of the mustard family. This diverse family includes weeds like stinkweed (with round, flat, seed pods), garden vegetables like broccoli and cabbage, and flowers such as alyssum. Almost all the mustards have the pungent watery juice that makes them so valuable as seasonings or salad greens.

There are nine rock cresses in Alberta, but they are difficult to identify, as you need both the fruits and the flowers, a hand lens and a fair amount of patience. Any time you see a small cross-shaped flower with a long narrow seed pod (sometimes round or heart-shaped), you can be fairly certain that you've found a mustard.

x 1

x 1

Prickly or Spotted Saxifrage *Saxifraga bronchialis*

One way of attracting insects to nectar is to have spotted nectar guides. Bees seem to be attracted to a broken pattern in the same way that contrasting colours attract them: it seems to be the contrast that is important. One of the ways that researchers learn the habits of bees is to place a flower or a painted image directly behind a sheet of glass. As the bees attempt to reach the nectar or pollen, their sticky tongues leave minute prints on the glass. Red flowers collect few tongue prints because the bees are not attracted to red. Spotted saxifrage would show tongue prints directly over the centre, where the bees are attracted by the broken-spot pattern.

White Mountain Avens *Dryas octopetala*

These white avens are truly alpine — you won't find them on low gravel bars like their yellow cousins, but instead on open turfy alpine slopes. The white avens is a 'soil maker.' It carpets a freshly-graveled alpine slope, making and saving soil beneath the thick mat of leaves. When a good bed of soil builds up, grasses, sedges and other flowers invade and slowly the avens die out, unable to compete in the new environment. Fossilized imprints have been found of Dryas leaves that are 10,000 years old. When the glaciers withdrew from the prairies and the mountains, they left behind miles of barren glacial gravel. The pioneer soil-builders that healed those ancient scars were the ancestors of these small avens.

Stonecrop *Sedum lanceolatum*

Beside bare grey rock silhouetted against fast-moving clouds, the wind whips your map from your hands and your hat from your head. At your feet, sheltered by a rock wall, is stonecrop. The small fat leaves feel waxy and smooth; their sap is a thick gummy liquid instead of the watery sap of most plants. This is a desert plant, closely related to the succulents growing in the Mexican deserts. The small leaves, thick sap and waxy covering all help to conserve water. The minimal snow cover, intense sunshine and high winds can whip moisture away faster than a mountain storm can brew, and the ability to conserve moisture by preventing evaporation is a key to success in this alpine desert.

Stonecrop is a perennial/biennial plant. The whole plant is a true perennial, living for many years. Each year new shoots sprout, some of which develop into a tight rosette of leaves before winter. The second year those shoots grow upright instead of creeping along the ground, producing flowers and then seeds. At the end of the year, the erect flowering stems die back, leaving a low creeping plant to survive the winter, hugging tightly to the rocks to stay out of the wind.

x 1

134

Golden Fleabane *Erigeron aureus*

This is not a common flower, but I included it because of the appeal of its sunny daisy face and its warm dark fur. The fur works just like the fur on animals. The long dark hairs trap the heat produced by the golden fleabane, holding it tight to the body of the plant and away from the cold fingers of the wind. On a sunny day, the fur shields the plant from the burning ultra violet rays of the sun, while at the same time absorbing the heat.

x 1

Glossary

Alkaloid A bitter alkaline substance frequently found in seed plants.
Anthocyanin Water soluble pigments; yellow, orange, red and blue.
Alternate Leaves borne singly along the stem, not opposite or whorled.
Anther The pollen-bearing part of the stamen.
Aspect The side of the mountain facing a given direction, i.e. the south aspect is the side facing south.
Basal Leaves clustered at the base of the plant.
Bog A wetland with still, acid water with moss peat underfoot.
Bract A small leaf included within, or at the base of a flower cluster. May be coloured, like aster or bracted lousewort.
Bulb An underground bud with thick fleshly scales that are stored with reserve food.
Bulbil A small bulb borne on a stem in place of a flower.
Chinook A warm, dry wind that blows down the eastern Rocky Mountain slopes across the prairies.
Clasping Where the base of a leaf splits and wraps partially around the stem.
Clone A group of genetically identical plants, usually produced by vegetative reproduction, such as runners or bulbils.
Complete A flower with petals, sepals, stamens and pistils.
Composite A flower in the daisy family, composed of many ray and/ or disc flowers.
Corm A swollen underground stem. Similar to a bulb, but solid not scaly.
Deciduous Leaves which drop in the fall; not evergreen.
Disc The central part of a composite flower like a daisy; composed of many tubular flowers.
Divided A leaf which is split to the centre vein or to the base, dividing it into distinct sections.
Drupe A fleshy fruit with a single large seed (pit) inside.
Entire A leaf with a continuous margin; i.e. not divided, toothed or lobed.
Evergreen A plant whose leaves remain green all year.
Fen A wetland of slow-moving, alkaline water with sedge peat underfoot.

Fruit The seed-bearing portion of a plant. May include a fleshy layer with many seeds (e.g. fairy bells), or a thin dry coat with a single seed inside (e.g. aster).

Fused Flower parts which are joined together making a bell, urn, slipper or cylinder.

Gene A part of a chromosome that governs the inheritance of a single characteristic.

Gland A structure (often a hair with a bulbous tip) which secretes nectar or volatile oils.

Head A short, dense, terminal cluster of flowers (e.g. golden fleabane).

Hummock A small hill or rounded mound.

Hybrid Plant or animal produced by crossing two different species.

Irregular Flowers in which the parts are obviously dissimilar in size or shape.

Keel The bottom two petals of a pea flower. They are joined together and look somewhat like the keel of a boat.

Krummholz Stunted trees growing at timberline.

Lance-shaped A leaf longer that it is wide, tapered at the end.

Larva The immature form of an insect. Frequently looks worm-like.

Latex The milky juice of certain plants (e.g. false dandelion).

Leaflet One of the sections of a divided leaf (e.g. strawberry or sweet vetch).

Legume A pea pod with no construction between the seeds. Also the name for plants in the pea family (e.g. milk vetch).

Lobe One of the segments of a leaf or flower, usually rounded. Not split as far as a divided leaf (e.g. Hooker's thistle).

Loment A pea pod with constrictions between the seeds (e.g. sweet vetch).

Marsh A wetland with seasonal flooding, thick mud and grasses.

Mycorrhizal fungi Soil fungi associated with the roots of a plant.

Narrow A leaf blade many times longer than wide (e.g. blue-eyed grass).

Nodule A small lump or swelling on the roots of a plant.

Open A flower with the flower parts lying more or less flat so that all parts can be seen (e.g. buttercup).

Opposite Leaves arranged in pairs on a stem.

Ovule A part of the ovary which, after fertilization, becomes the seed.

Parasite A plant or animal which lives in or on another living organism.

Photosynthesis The process by which green plants change light energy into carbohydrates.

Pistil The central female reproductive part of a flower, including stigma, style, and ovary.

Pollen The male spores produced by the anther.

Ray The petal-like flowers on a composite flower (e.g. aster).

Regular A flower with all petals or sepals the same shape and size.

Rhizome A horizontal underground stem (e.g. star-flowered Solomon's-seal).

Rosette A circular cluster of leaves at the base of the stem (e.g. sweet-flowered androcase).

Spur A hollow tubular projection on a flower. Frequently holds nectar (e.g. white bog orchid).

Stamen The male, pollen bearing organ of a flower. It includes the stalk and the anther.

Stolon A horizontal branch from the base of a plant, producing new plants at the tip. A runner (e.g. strawberry).

Tendril A slender, twining portion of a leaf or stem (e.g. vetch).

Toothed A leaf having many small indentations along the edges (e.g. rose).

Umbel A flower cluster in which all the flower stalks radiate from the same point (e.g. cow parsnip).

Urn A flower shaped like a round vase with a narrow neck (e.g. red heath).

Volatile A chemical which evaporates easily.

Wing One of the two side petals of a pea flower.

Whorl Several leaves attached at a single spot on a stem (e.g. bedstraw).

Reading List

Brown, Annora. *Old Man's Garden*. Evergreen Press Ltd. Vancouver, 1970. Tales of plants and people beautifully illustrated with block prints. A book to curl up with in front of a fire. Out of print, but you may be able to find it in a library.

Gadd, Ben. *Handbook of the Canadian Rockies*. Corax Press, Jasper, Alberta, 1986. An all-purpose book covering history, geology, plants, animals, birds and insects. An engaging and easy writing style.

Kuijt, Job. *A Flora of Waterton Lakes National Park*. University of Alberta Press, 1982. Good for Banff and Jasper. Technical book with keys and simple line drawings. Easier to use than Moss.

Meeuse, Bastiaan and Sean Morris. *The Sex Life of Plants*. Facts on File, New York, 1984. Based on PBS Nature series. A table-top book full of glossy photos and lots of information on pollination by a leading researcher. Very good.

Moss, E. H. *Flora of Alberta*. 2nd Edition revised by J. C. Packer. U. of Toronto Press, 1983. The standard text for Alberta botanists. Keys and maps but no pictures. (All Latin names were taken from this text.)

Porsild, A. E. *Rocky Mountain Wild Flowers*. University of Toronto Press. A beautiful book of 250 watercolours. Plants are grouped in botanical families and there is no key — lots of page flipping.

Scotter, George W. and Halle Flygare. *Wildflowers of the Canadian Rockies*. Hurtig Publishers, Edmonton, 1986. Photographs and descriptions of over 200 species arranged by colour.

Watts, May Thielgaard. *Reading the Landscape of America*. Collier Books, N. Y., 1975. Another 'fireplace' book on basic ecology: by a wonderful story-teller and an outstanding ecologist.

Zwinger, A. and B. E. Willard. *Land above the Trees*. A guide to American Alpine Tundra. Harper and Row, 1986. Well-researched and easy to read.

Index

141

The Author / Illustrator

C. Dana Bush is a self-employed writer and illustrator with particular interest in native plants and conservation issues. She was educated at the University of Calgary (B.Sc. in Plant Biology), S.A.I.T., and the Alberta College of Art. She is a member of numerous horticultural, environmental and conservation groups, including the Alberta Native Plant Council. She lives in Calgary.